Contents

Introduction
Changing the way we feel   **4**

1 Tobacco, caffeine and alcohol
Legal drugs   **14**

2 Solvents and nitrites
Dangerous vapours   **24**

3 Anabolic steroids
Seeking super-fitness   **27**

4 Tranquillizers and sedatives
Uses and abuses   **30**

5 Cannabis
Sedative weed   **34**

6 Ecstasy
Happiness with a price   **40**

7 Cocaine and amphetamines
Stimulant effects   **44**

8 LSD and other hallucinogens
The 'mind expanders'   **50**

9 Heroin and morphine
Drugs from the opium poppy   **54**

Glossary   **60**

Resources   **62**

Index   **63**

Introduction
Changing the way we feel

'When I sniff,
I'm not hungry, I forget.
Sniffing takes me away from this place.'
(Juan, aged 12, Mexican street
child who sniffs
solvents)

A drug is a chemical that enters your body and changes your physical or mental state. Drugs have always been in use to relieve the pain of illness or to change the way we feel. Drugs are part of our heritage, figuring heavily in myths and religions. From the water of magical wells that could cure all ills to the latest wonder drug from a pharmaceutical company, drugs are tied up with people's desire to change the way things are, to feel better.

When drugs are given or taken in order to cure or relieve the symptoms or effects of an illness or injury, we say that they are being used 'therapeutically'. But people also take drugs to achieve an altered mood or state, or to improve performance. The drugs that people use in these

Chewing coca

A miner in Bolivia chews the leaves of the coca plant as his ancestors have for thousands of years. Coca leaves are processed and refined to produce the profoundly addictive drug cocaine.

Traditions

Throughout history drugs have been used all over the world and in all cultures. Each region has its own drugs. Opium from the opium poppy originally came from Asia and the Middle East. Magic Mushrooms (psilocybin) are native to northern Europe and were used for their mind-altering properties in pagan religious rites. The leaves of the coca plant were traditionally chewed by many native South American tribes for their ability to improve attention and alertness and the feelings of wellbeing they impart. Some Native American tribes traditionally used mescalin during their religious rites, as a window into the world of the spirit.

DRUGS

Sarah Lennard-Brown

W

HODDER
Wayland

an imprint of Hodder Children's Books

© 2001 White-Thomson Publishing Ltd

White-Thomson Publishing Ltd,
2-3 St Andrew's Place, Lewes,
East Sussex BN7 1UP

Published in Great Britain in 2001 by Hodder Wayland, an imprint of Hodder Children's Books

This paperback edition published in 2004
This book was produced for White-Thomson Publishing Ltd by Ruth Nason.

Design: Carole Binding
Picture research: Glass Onion Pictures

British Library Cataloguing in Publication Data
Lennard-Brown, Sarah
    Drugs. - (Health Issues)
    1. Drugs - Physiological effect
    2. Drug abuse
    I. Title
    613.8'3

ISBN 0 7502 3538 1

Printed in China

Hodder Children's Books
A division of Hodder Headline Limited
338 Euston Road, London NW1 3BH

Acknowledgements

The author and publishers thank the following for their permission to reproduce photographs and illustrations: John Birdsall Photography: page 59; Camera Press: cover and pages 1, 5; Corbis Images: pages 4 (Jeremy Horner), 20 (Macduff Everton), 27 (Reuters NewMedia Inc.), 29t (Neal Preston), 30t (Jean-Pierre Lescourret), 49 (Nathan Benn), 58 (Annie Griffiths Belt); Angela Hampton Family Life Pictures: pages 8, 13; Impact Photos: pages 18 (Dominic Sansoni), 36 (Daniel White), 38 (Peter Arkell), 54 (Piers Cavendish); Photofusion: pages 11 (David Montford), 22 (Emma Smith), 33t (Mark Campbell), 33b (Brian Mitchell), 35 (David Montford); Popperfoto: pages 17, 23, 24, 27, 29b, 30b, 37, 39, 40, 42, 43, 55, 56; Chris Schwarz: page 51; Science Photo Library: pages 15 (A. Glauberman), 16 (Jim Selby), 34 (James King-Holmes), 46 (Pascal Goetgheluck), 50 (Sinclair Stammers), 54 (National Library of Medicine); Tony Stone Images: page 14 (Martin Rogers); Topham Picturepoint: pages 10, 21 (Bob Daemmrich/The Image Works), 44, 47 (John Griffin/TIW), 52; Wayland Picture Library: pages 7, 28.

Injecting heroin
Teenagers get ready to inject heroin in an abandoned building in St Petersburg, Russia.

'recreational' ways range from alcohol and tobacco through to substances like heroin, which are invaluable when used in a medical context but can wreck the lives of people who become dependent on them for any pleasure.

'I feel strong. I can fight anything. No one can mess with me, no one.'
(Christoph, aged 14, gang member, about using crack cocaine)

The psychoactive effects of drugs

The drugs that people take for their mood-altering, or psychoactive, effects fall into three broad categories:

⚬ Stimulants
⚬ Depressants or sedatives
⚬ Hallucinogenic drugs

Stimulants are drugs that increase energy and activity levels. They are often described as drugs that 'hype you up'. Depressants and sedatives, on the other hand, decrease energy and activity levels; they 'calm you down'. Hallucinogenic drugs alter the way you see the world. Their effect can range from changing the way you see colours or hear sounds to making you see things that are not there at all. The experience of hallucinating is often referred to as 'tripping' or 'mind-bending'.

'I forget that I'm too fat or I haven't finished my essay or my boyfriend's chatting up my best friend. For a few hours I feel perfect.'
(Carla, aged 17, about why she uses ecstasy)

How drugs work

A drug may be introduced into the body by swallowing, smoking, inhaling or injecting. Once in the body it is absorbed into the blood. Some is filtered out by the liver, which removes toxins from the body. The rest passes into the brain where it acts on the areas called synapses, where nerves pass messages to other nerves.

Nerves communicate with each other by passing minute amounts of chemicals between the end of one nerve and the beginning of the next nerve. When nerve A is stimulated, a chemical (called a neurostransmitter) is released from the end of it and passes across a tiny gap to nerve B. Nerve B has special areas called receptors, which pick up neurotransmitters and, if enough receptors are filled with the neuro-transmitter, then nerve B will send the message along to the next nerve in line. There are very many different neurotransmitters, each linked to a group of nerves that do a particular job, such as moving your fingers or experiencing the pain of stepping on a pin.

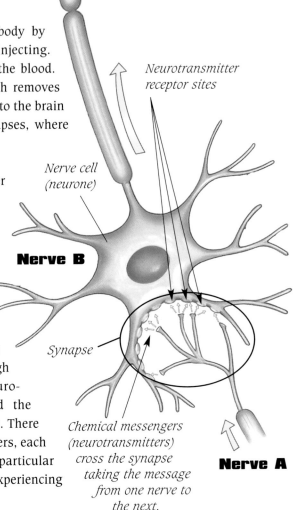

Neurotransmitter receptor sites

Nerve cell (neurone)

Nerve B

Synapse

Chemical messengers (neurotransmitters) cross the synapse taking the message from one nerve to the next.

Nerve A

Different drugs work either by blocking receptors and preventing them doing their normal job or by mimicking a naturally occurring chemical in the brain (neurotransmitter) and so increasing the nerve's activity.

Most drugs are eventually metabolized (broken down) by the liver and leave the body through the kidneys and intestines by the processes of excretion. The speed at which a drug is metabolized determines how long its effects last. A drug that is metabolized very quickly will have only a short effect. Some drugs, such as cannabis,

Chemical messengers

Psychoactive drugs work either by blocking the receptor sites, so that messages cannot be transmitted from one nerve to the next, or by increasing the concentration of neurotransmitters at the synapse, so increasing the numbers of messages sent.

Blood supply
Once absorbed into your blood, drugs are rapidly transported all over your body.

are metabolized into other chemicals that are also psychoactive and so their effect continues for quite a long time. It is very hard to change the rate at which a drug is metabolized, so once you have taken a drug you cannot easily hurry recovery. Cocaine is metabolized quickly, which accounts for the sudden 'high' followed by a crash. This contributes to the drug's addictiveness, as the crash is so horrible that the user wants to take more of the drug to stop it.

As you continue to use a drug, you develop tolerance. This means that your body gets used to the drug and acts to minimize the damage it causes. Your liver builds up large amounts of the chemicals needed to break down the drug. The result is that you get rid of the drug more quickly, and need to take more of the drug to get the same effect as before. The more frequently a drug is taken and the higher the dose, the more likely it is for tolerance to develop.

When you take a drug, your body adapts to minimize the damage from it. Therefore, when you stop taking a drug, your body has to adapt to normality again. This is called withdrawal. So, if you are taking a stimulant, your body acts to restore balance by increasing its production of calming/depressing neurochemicals. Once the stimulant is removed, the body has to rebalance but until it does, there will be an overabundance of calming/depressing neuro-chemicals in your brain and you will feel sleepy and low.

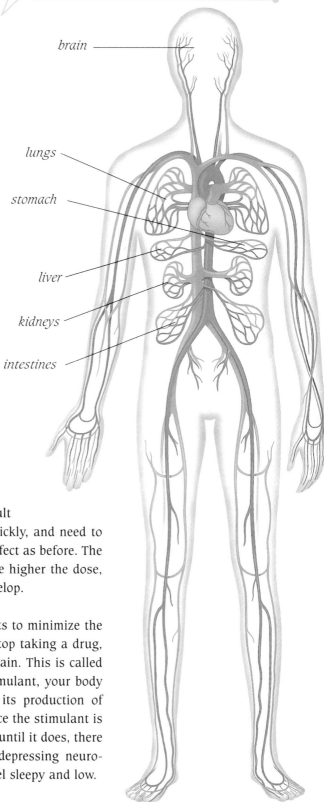

brain

lungs

stomach

liver

kidneys

intestines

The effect of drugs on health

People take drugs for many reasons. These include curiosity, pressure from friends, revenge (perhaps on parents or teachers), daring (wanting to do something illegal), boredom, addiction, or to experience their effects. However, drugs are powerful chemicals and have long-term as well as short-term effects.

Drugs are often thought of as 'magic bullets'. People think that, when they take a drug, it does what they expect it to and nothing else. This is rarely the case. As we have seen, when you take a drug it is absorbed into the bloodstream and taken all over the body. Some of its effects can be pleasurable and some can be damaging.

'Out of it'
This girl is not enjoying the short-term effects of the drugs she has taken.

According to the World Health Organization (WHO), drug dependence was the direct cause of 5,000 deaths worldwide in 1999; and alcohol dependence was the direct cause of 60,000 deaths. These figures are slightly misleading as they do not include deaths from diseases spread by taking drugs, such as hepatitis or HIV, or deaths where drugs were a contributing factor but which are classified under other headings such as suicide, accidental poisoning, accidental death or road traffic accidents.

Many accidental poisonings occur as a result of mixing drugs. Drugs that are not usually lethal can become so if they are mixed with other drugs – particularly cold remedies or alcohol. Unfortunately, this is very easy to do. The amount of a drug taken is also important. An overdose of a drug at the very least will make you feel terrible and at the worst can kill. How much of a drug you need to take to overdose depends on what drug it is, how strong it is and how much tolerance you have developed to it.

Addiction

Addiction involves the repetitive and compulsive use of a substance despite its negative consequences. Addiction is often categorized as physical (to do with the body) or psychological (to do with the mind). Different people often use these words to mean different things, but in this book psychological addiction involves forming a habit and physical addiction involves your brain or body undergoing changes which mean that the drug becomes necessary for your body to function normally.

Gambling is sometimes described as psychologically addictive. It is compulsive, despite the negative consequences on your bank balance, but it does not change the way your body works. Some drugs are addictive in this way. For example, cannabis is not known to change the way your body works, but using it can become a habit that is hard to break. Anyone who has ever tried to stop biting their nails will understand how difficult it can be to break a habit.

Physically addictive drugs change the way your body works. The effect can be mild: for example, if you are addicted to coffee, you may experience headaches for a few days when you stop drinking it. Or it can be severe: for example, when you are addicted to cocaine, your body stops producing a neurotransmitter called dopamine. The drug replaces the neurotransmitter. As you need dopamine to experience pleasure and contentment, if you are addicted to cocaine and then stop taking it, you are unable to experience any pleasure until your brain heals and starts producing dopamine again.

Physically addictive substances activate groups of nerves in your brain that

Treating addiction

Treatment usually involves taking the user right away from their normal environment and helping them to withdraw safely under medical supervision. Once they have detoxified, they are encouraged to join counselling or support groups where they learn strategies to resist temptation and find help to stay drug-free. Treating addiction is a long process; cravings for the drug can last for many months, sometimes your whole life.

respond to normal pleasures such as food, sex and love. Scientists have shown that animals and humans will do an incredible variety of things to stimulate these nerves (sometimes called 'reward circuits'). For example, if the nerves that control pleasure in an animal are stimulated by a gentle electric current, the animal will push levers, run treadmills, and do anything within its power to keep turning the current on.

The neurotransmitter dopamine seems to be closely connected with our experience of pleasure, and substances that are addictive usually have a direct effect on the production of dopamine. Addiction usually develops slowly. People do not get addicted the first time they try a drug. The changes happen gradually. Eventually the drug takes over the experience of pleasure completely, so that when there is no drug the reward circuits don't work. Addicts no longer get pleasure from food, warmth or love, only the drug. Being unable to feel pleasure without a drug is a powerful reason for keeping on taking it.

Although physical addiction usually develops slowly, some drugs are more addictive than others and some people are more likely than others to become addicted. The reason that addiction can be faster with certain types of drug is again due to pleasure and reward circuits. Some drugs are simply more pleasurable and have fewer immediate negative effects. The fact that they are so pleasurable means that they have an enormous effect on the brain. It also makes it more likely that they will be used often and so addiction can develop quickly.

So why do some people get addicted and not others? Recent research seems to suggest that there may be a part of our genetic make-up that can make us more likely to

'Who needs drugs? We're high on life!'

become addicted. Studies of alcoholics and their children have shown some differences in brain wave pattern. Animal studies seem to support this idea, but the responsible genes have not yet been fully mapped out. However, having a genetic vulnerability to addiction does not mean that you are inevitably going to become an addict. Similarly, not having the gene does not necessarily mean that you will not become an addict. Environment, behaviour, circumstance and free will all have a part to play.

The term 'addictive personality' is often talked about in magazines, though what exactly is an 'addictive personality' is not clear. It appears that people with a tendency to be obsessive find it harder to break addiction, and people who are risk takers and impulsive are more likely to try a drug in the first place. However, these impulses may be channelled into safer things such as tidying up or rock climbing.

Where you live and who you live or work with *do* affect your risk of becoming addicted to drugs. You are more likely to become an addict if you grow up in a household with a substance-abusing parent, if your friends abuse drugs, or if you have been abused as a child. Early experimentation with tobacco, cannabis and alcohol also increase your chances of addiction.

Environmental factors can also help people resist addiction. These include loving supportive family and friends, stable secure life, no family history of substance abuse and a good education. However, it must be remembered that anyone can become addicted to drugs, no matter who they are or where they live.

'I don't want to take drugs.
I've got too much to lose.
Why risk it all for a quick thrill?'
(Jay, computer programmer)

Issues for society

Taking drugs can have an impact not only on your health but also on the way you live your life and on the society you live in. Laws protect people from drugs. They usually categorize drugs according to how harmful and addictive they are. The more harmful a drug, the higher the penalties for producing, supplying or using it. Taking illegal drugs means that you break the law; you may be arrested and, if prosecuted, risk prison or at least a criminal record. This can make it very difficult to go to college or get a job.

In many countries it is also an offence to allow illegal drugs to be taken on your property. So, if the police discover your drugs in your parents' home, your parents can be prosecuted and sent to prison. The effect that drugs have on you can also spoil your relationships. People may notice a change in your behaviour or personality. Drugs can make you aggressive, sleepy, or sometimes just strange. For people who love you, these changes will be worrying, difficult to live with and very stressful.

Drugs also affect the amount of crime in our society. We often hear of big drugs 'busts' at customs, where people are caught trying to smuggle illegal drugs into a country, or of the scandal of drug 'bosses' in far-away countries who profit from the sale of illegal drugs and live in well-protected luxury. But by far the biggest cost to society from the use of drugs is related to smaller-scale crimes, such as burglary, assault, mugging, prostitution and criminal damage. It costs money to buy drugs and drug addiction can be very expensive. For many addicts life consists of a never-ending cycle of committing a crime to get money for drugs, taking the drugs, being 'out of it' for a while and then getting more money for more drugs before withdrawal symptoms start.

Risks – The facts

- *You can never be sure exactly what you are taking.*

- *Drugs are often mixed with other things such as talcum powder to dilute the drug and increase the profit for the dealer.*

- *You do not know how pure a substance is, so it is easy to overdose.*

- *You can't be sure what effect the drug will have on you, even if you have taken it before.*

- *Mixing drugs is very dangerous, especially with alcohol or cold medicines.*

- *Sharing needles and syringes carries serious risk of infection from diseases like HIV and hepatitis.*

- *There is a real risk of being caught by the police. You may be arrested and prosecuted.*

- *There is a real risk to other members of your family. Your parents may be arrested and charged if drugs are found in their home.*

- *You run the risk of becoming addicted if you take an addictive drug.*

Drugs get a lot of media coverage. Some people think this is good: that you are less likely to try illegal drugs if you are scared of them. Others think that the reporting of drug-related news has gone too far, that scare stories glamorize drugs and so encourage young people to try them. The most abused drugs are alcohol and tobacco, which are legal in most countries. Despite the lower price and increased availability of illegal drugs, the vast majority of people will never take them. Illegal drugs are not part of normal life and of those who do try them, most do not continue using them or progress to becoming addicts.

Staying in control

It is a good idea to think about drugs and the situations you might find yourself in before they happen. If someone offered you a cannabis cigarette, what would you do? If you want to try it, are you fully aware of the risks you are taking? Do you know what you are being offered? If you don't want to take it, how will you say no? One way of practising saying no is to do some role-play. If you do this with a friend, you can discuss alternative ways of handling situations. Try role-playing these:

- You are standing outside a club and a friend asks if you would like to try an ecstasy tablet.
- A friend has had too much to drink and someone offers them a tablet.
- A friend has taken an unknown tablet at a club and is behaving strangely.

This book

The following chapters investigate the most commonly abused drugs, looking at their history, chemistry, why people use them, their short-term and long-term effects and particular issues surrounding their use in the modern world. The drugs are presented in related groups. Cannabis and ecstasy have chapters to themselves as they are probably the most widely used illegal drugs at present.

Role-play

It is impossible to say exactly what to do in any situation you role-play because your life, experience and environment are different from everyone else's.

1 Tobacco, caffeine and alcohol
Legal drugs

Tobacco, caffeine and alcohol are three legal drugs that many people use every day. They are not necessarily less addictive, less powerful or less potentially harmful than many illegal drugs.

Tobacco

Tobacco has been smoked, chewed or sniffed for hundreds of years. Christopher Columbus took the tobacco plant from the 'New World' back to Europe in the fifteenth century and from then on the use of tobacco gradually increased. By the seventeenth century pipe-smoking was popular. Taking snuff became fashionable around the beginning of the eighteenth century, followed by smoking cigars in the nineteenth century. The cigarette was invented in the mid-nineteenth century but only became popular between the First and Second World Wars.

Why smoke?

The effect of tobacco depends on the mental and physical state of the person taking it. Sometimes it can act as a stimulant and at other times it can feel relaxing.

Chemicals in tobacco

Tobacco smoke contains more than 4,000 chemicals. These include:

- ⦿ *nicotine – a stimulant*
- ⦿ *tar – a mixture of chemicals including formaldehyde, arsenic, cyanide, benzene, toluene*
- ⦿ *carbon monoxide gas – which prevents the body absorbing essential oxygen from the air. Without oxygen we cannot live.*

Effects of using tobacco

SHORT-TERM	LONG-TERM
Relaxation	Breathlessness
Stimulation	Chronic lung disease
Feelings of pleasure	Lung cancer
Fast pulse	Increased risk of other cancers (especially throat and mouth)
Nausea	Increased risk of heart disease
Raised blood pressure	Faster skin aging
Increased production of mucus	Stained fingers and teeth
	Slower healing of wounds
	Major health risks to unborn babies of mothers who smoke
	Craving

Tobacco contains many chemicals that affect your body. However, the main addictive component is nicotine. This chemical is as addictive as heroin or cocaine. It affects your brain by acting on the production of dopamine, which plays an important role in the way we experience pleasure. Taking nicotine results in the brain releasing a rush of dopamine, which is pleasurable. However, long-term use of nicotine affects the brain's ability to produce dopamine naturally, and so the user ends up being dependent on nicotine in order to be able to feel happy.

Smoker's lung
A smoker's misshapen lung (right) is darker and rougher than the lung of a non-smoker (left).

Smoking tobacco has a poor effect on health. It is associated with the development of many long-term diseases such as lung disease, cancer and heart disease. It has been estimated that in 1998 cigarette consumption accounted for 4,023,000 deaths and 49,288,000 lives disabled by disease worldwide. The World Health

Organization (WHO) estimates that this number will rise to 10 million deaths per year by 2030.

Because nicotine is so addictive, it can be hard for people to stop smoking. However, the evidence suggests that, once you have stopped, the likelihood of suffering from a disease caused by smoking drops dramatically.

'Within a week of giving up smoking, I stopped coughing. By two weeks, I began to be able to run for the bus. It's fantastic.'
(Sam, bank clerk)

On-going debates

Some people feel that nicotine is such a dangerous drug that it should be made illegal. There is an on-going debate about whether it is right to allow advertising of cigarettes and tobacco-related products. As the popularity of smoking decreases in the richer countries, the tobacco companies are trying to increase their sales and profits by promoting cigarettes in the developing world. Developing countries have little money to spare for educating people about the risks of smoking.

Tobacco also affects developing countries in other ways. Most of the world's tobacco crop is grown in these countries and, as it is susceptible to diseases, it requires the use of large amounts of pesticides. This can have an impact on the local environment, threatening wildlife and native plants. There are also reports of forest clearance in order to grow tobacco, and this is thought to contribute to global warming.

Nicotine patch
A nicotine patch supplies a small amount of nicotine through the skin to help lessen withdrawal symptoms as you give up smoking.

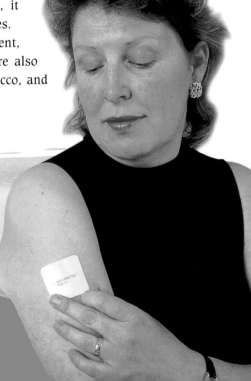

Withdrawal

Symptoms of withdrawal from tobacco include:

Irritability/aggression	Light-headedness
Craving	Restlessness
Increased appetite	Depression
Poor concentration	Night-time awakenings

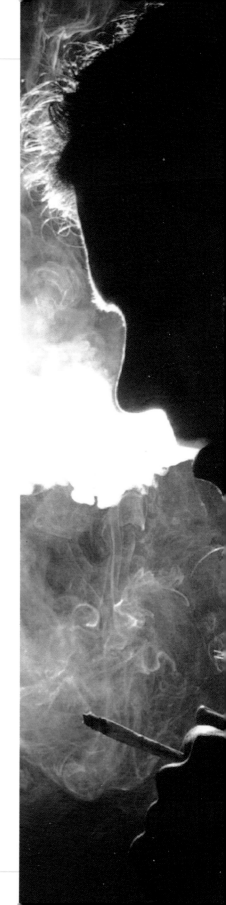

Who should bear the cost of treatment for tobacco-related illnesses is also hotly debated. Some people feel that these illnesses are self-inflicted and that smokers should be responsible for paying for their own treatment. Others believe that tobacco is so addictive that, once hooked, people cannot help using it and that they should be entitled to the same health care as everyone else.

There have recently been high-profile court cases in Britain and the USA where people have sued the tobacco companies for making addictive products and conspiring to hide the dangers of smoking.

Passive smoking

Passive smoking occurs when people who are not smokers are in the same room as or close by to people who are smoking. The tobacco smoke passes into the air around the smoker and is inhaled by everyone nearby.

The World Health Organization states that passive smoking is associated with an increased risk of lung cancer in adults, but that children are most severely affected. Children are at a much higher risk of suffering from severe lung conditions such as asthma and bronchitis if they live with people who smoke. Passive smoking has also been implicated in sudden infant death syndrome, low birth weight and intrauterine growth retardation (the poor development of babies in the womb).

During the late twentieth century concern over passive smoking increased. Many people felt angry that their health, and the health of their children, was being put at risk. This concern resulted in smoking being banned from many public places across Western Europe and the USA. However, some people believe that the risks of passive smoking have been exaggerated. Over recent years there have been protests from groups of smokers and the tobacco industry who feel that their freedom is being curtailed by smoking bans and that these are unnecessary.

Picking tea

Tea is grown on plantations in India and the Far East. Its history is thought to begin in China, in the fourth century, when it was regarded as a medicinal herb. It was imported to Europe by the fifteenth century, as a medicine.

Caffeine

Caffeine is the chemical name for a stimulant found in tea, coffee, chocolate, soft caffeinated drinks, many cough and cold remedies and some over-the-counter pain relievers. A low dose of caffeine can make you feel more alert and capable. A high dose will make you nervous and agitated. Caffeine poisoning makes you feel sick, confused and shaky. It also causes a rapid and irregular heartbeat.

Effects of taking caffeine

SHORT-TERM	LONG-TERM (more than 500 mg per day)
Enhanced physical performance	Raised cholesterol level (non-filtered coffee)
Stimulates breathing	Fast and irregular heartbeat
Increased heart rate	Possible increase in risk of heart disease
Raised blood pressure	Raised blood pressure
Increase in urine production	Nervous agitation
Relaxation of bowel	Restlessness
Stomach irritation	Nausea
Sleeplessness	Increased stress response
Increased alertness	Stomach irritation
Headaches	Decreased female fertility
	Low birth-weight babies

Caffeine works by blocking the action of a chemical in the brain called adenosine. Adenosine has a calming and sedative action on the brain and so taking caffeine has the effect of increasing the brain's activity. You can develop a mild tolerance to caffeine but this is quickly reversed. The withdrawal effects are minor, usually involving headache and fatigue for up to a week, and although people enjoy and sometimes rely on the drug, it is not classed as addictive by most authorities.

Coffee

Coffee was first imported to Europe from Yemen in the sixteenth century.

Chocolate

Chocolate became popular in the nineteenth century when the Dutch developed the chocolate bar.
A 100g bar of dark chocolate contains about the same amount of caffeine as a cup of percolator brewed coffee (approximately 80 milligrams).

Caffeine in common products

PRODUCT	CAFFEINE (mg)
Filtered Robusta coffee (200 ml)	150
Filtered Arabica coffee (200 ml)	100
Instant coffee (200 ml)	65
Decaffeinated coffee (200 ml)	3
Cup of tea brewed for 5 minutes	100
Cup of tea brewed for 1 minute	30
Coca-Cola (200ml)	46
Dr Pepper (200ml)	46
Pepsi-Cola (200 ml)	38
Over-the-counter cold remedies	16-30
Over-the-counter pain relievers	30-65
Over-the-counter stimulants	100-200

Alcohol

There is evidence that humans have been using alcohol for 6,000 years or more. During the Middle Ages and Tudor period in Britain, weak beer was the staple drink of young and old, rich and poor. In modern times, alcohol has become the most popular drug in the world. It is powerful, and poisonous in large quantities.

Alcohol is a depressant drug. When you drink it, you initially feel relaxed. You may lose some inhibitions and become chatty and friendly. With more alcohol you gradually become uncoordinated, with slurred speech; you may become aggressive or sad and tearful. Finally, you may become unconscious and there is a risk that, if you vomit whilst unconscious, you could inhale the vomit and suffocate. If someone who has been drinking heavily becomes unconscious and has breathing difficulties, they need medical attention quickly.

Long-term abuse of alcohol can lead to conditions such as cirrhosis of the liver, heart disease, pancreatitis, stomach

Ethanol

The chemical name for the alcohol in beer, wine and spirits is ethanol. Ethanol is easily absorbed into the blood, and quickly affects nearly every part of the body.

problems and brain damage. However, there does seem to be some evidence that mild to moderate alcohol intake (1–2 glasses of wine, or 1 pint of beer per day for adult women; and 2-3 glasses of wine or 1-2 pints of beer per day for men) may have some positive effects on health. It seems that drinks like red wine may contain substances that help prevent heart disease, provided that they are drunk in moderation.

Effects of using alcohol

FEW SOCIAL DRINKS
Happiness
Relaxation
Loss of inhibition
Impaired fine motor
    coordination
Impaired judgement
Impaired reaction time
Increased risk of accidents

BINGE DRINKING
Hangover (headache,
    nausea, vomiting)
Impotence ('Brewer's
    droop')
Decreased sperm count
Stomach upset
Liver damage
Pancreas damage
Memory loss
Aggression/depression
Risks to unborn child
Unconsciousness
Risk of death from
    alcohol poisoning or
    inhaling vomit
Increased risk of accidents

CHRONIC LONG-TERM USE
Reduction in brain size
Problems with short-term
    memory
Difficulty with thought
    processes
Difficulty problem-solving
Poor attention
Poor concentration
Impotence
Decreased sperm count
Alcohol-induced dementia
Fetal alcohol syndrome
Liver damage – jaundice,
    cirrhosis, cancer
Pancreas damage
Heart disease
High blood pressure
Stomach and digestive
    problems

Too close
*Alcohol can make
you lose the ability
to judge the effect
of your behaviour.*

Problem drinking
Alcohol causes a decrease in brain activity and memory difficulties.

Alcohol affects areas of your brain called 'neuronal receptors', particularly GABA and glutamate receptors. These areas are responsible for calming and exciting your brain cells. Alcohol works by increasing the action of the calming GABA receptors and decreasing the excitement of the glutamate receptors. This results in less brain activity and reduced ability to form new memories.

Alcohol also causes the brain to produce more of the chemical dopamine which helps us to experience pleasure. However the level of dopamine in your brain drops as the level of alcohol drops and this encourages you to drink more to experience pleasure again. This process is addictive. Alcohol is a very addictive drug and anyone can become addicted to it. Factors that increase your risk of becoming addicted include drinking more than three or four alcoholic drinks a day, having a relative who is an alcoholic and being male.

Withdrawal

Symptoms of withdrawal from alcohol include:

profound anxiety
tremors (shaking)
sleep disturbance
hallucinations
seizures (fits)
stomach cramps.

Withdrawing from long-term alcohol abuse can be very dangerous. The brain quickly builds up a tolerance to alcohol, increasing the activity and excitement of brain cells to compensate for the depressant effect of the drug.

This means that when you stop using alcohol your brain becomes very over-excited. This can result in fits, which can be life-threatening. Withdrawal from long-term alcohol abuse therefore needs to be medically supervised.

Alcohol and violence

A big issue facing western societies today is the relationship between alcohol and violence. People who have been drinking lose their inhibitions and sense of judgement. This can result in them becoming aggressive. This is a particular problem when groups of young men get together and drink alcohol at places like football matches or pubs and clubs. Alcohol is also implicated in self-inflicted violence, with four out of every ten male and three out of every ten female cases of suicide being associated with alcohol use.

Football violence
Alcohol reduces people's inhibitions and impairs their judgement. This can result in violent outbursts when alcohol is drunk at events like football matches.

Smashed to pieces

I hate alcohol. I'm never ever going to touch it. It's poison. It ruins everything, all smashed to pieces. My mum drinks, at least she used to. She was out of it all the time. I used to have to put her to bed, clear up. She's stopped now. She says she stopped because she loves me, but I don't know if it will be enough to keep her sober. I hope so. I don't want to lose her, but I don't want to live like that. It makes me so mad. I will never ever get like that.
(Jade, 16 years old)

2 Solvents and nitrites
Dangerous vapours

Solvents are a category of drugs including just about every industrial chemical that produces a vapour. They are extremely toxic when inhaled and often lethal. Sniffing these substances became popular because they were easier to obtain than other drugs and gave the same mood-altering effects. Glue sniffing became a recognized problem by the 1950s, reached its maximum popularity in the late 1970s and early 1980s and then went out of fashion.

Solvents

COMMON NAMES	CHEMICAL NAMES
Liquid petroleum gas	Butane gas, propane gas
Glues	
Fuels	Petrol/gasoline
Coolants	Toluene
Propellants	Chloroform
Paints	Volatile hydrocarbons
Nail polish and remover	
Antifreeze	Freon

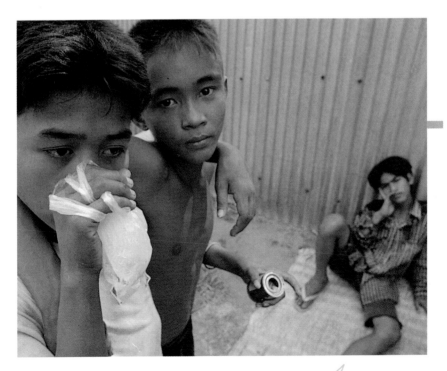

Glue sniffing
Street children sniffing glue in Phnom Penh, the capital of Cambodia, 1999.

CHAPTER 2

Inhaling the vapour from solvents produces the same sort of effect as alcohol; you feel uninhibited and get a 'rush'. This is quickly followed by depression, loss of control of body movements, changes in perception of time and space, plus delusions or hallucinations. You can also get ringing in the ears, stomach pains, reddening of the skin, vomiting, and heart and breathing problems.

Sniffing solvents can lead quickly to 'sudden sniffing death'. It is thought that solvents slow down the cells that set the beating rate of your heart whilst increasing their sensitivity to adrenalin (which makes the heart beat faster). This means that your heart tries simultaneously to slow down and to speed up. These confusing commands can cause your heart to stop beating altogether and death quickly follows.

Effects of inhaling solvents

SHORT-TERM
Loss of inhibitions
Exhilaration
Visual disturbances and hallucinations
Vomiting
Loss of coordination
Fast pulse
Abnormal heart rhythms
High risk of accidents, burns and suicide

OVERDOSE AND LONG-TERM
Dangerously poisonous
'Sudden sniffing death'

Long-term use damages central nervous system, heart, lungs, kidneys, liver, blood.

The long-term health effects of sniffing solvents are unclear, for several reasons. First, people who use them also use a lot of other drugs. Second, there is a high death rate among people who abuse solvents. And third, there are so many solvents that it is difficult to know which disease goes with which solvent. However, users who survive to become long-term abusers of solvents tend to end up with central nervous system damage plus damage to nearly every other system in the body.

'The sniffers round here all look stupid. I mean what's cool about sitting in a bus shelter with your head in a plastic bag?' (Andrew, student)

Many users are injured or killed in accidents that occur whilst intoxicated. Others die from suicide, though it is not clear whether people become suicidal due to solvent abuse or take solvents because they are feeling suicidal. About

20 per cent of deaths caused by solvent abuse are of first-time users.

Nitrites

Nitrites (amyl nitrite and butyl nitrite) are a group of flammable yellow liquids with a fruity smell. Inhaling them relaxes the smooth muscles of the body, which means that the blood vessels enlarge and your blood pressure falls, the pupils get bigger, letting more light into the eyes, and the muscles controlling the anus and bladder relax – resulting in your passing urine or opening your bowels.

'You can usually tell when people have poppers at parties. There's this fruity smell, a bit like fruit drops, and they're very red in the face.'
(Nina, drugs education unit)

The drugs were developed in 1897 to treat heart conditions such as angina; by quickly enlarging blood vessels in the heart, they would relieve angina pain. But doctors found that they did not provide lasting relief and were unreliable. Nitrites are still used in the diagnosis and treatment of some heart conditions, but they are no longer generally prescribed for angina.

Inhaling nitrites produces a feeling of warmth, relaxation and a 'rush', which includes a fast heartbeat and exhilaration. The drug is also supposed to cause anal relaxation, and therefore assist anal intercourse. This is one of the main reasons why the drug is sometimes sold at sex shops, and why it is said to be popular with homosexual men. It is sometimes wafted around the room at parties. When nitrites are used recreationally, they are often referred to as 'poppers'.

It is possible to develop tolerance to nitrite drugs and withdrawal symptoms include headaches and heart problems. Nitrites are dangerously toxic if eaten or if the user has a blood circulation problem. They can also cause rashes if they come into contact with skin, and eye problems or even blindness if they are splashed into the eyes.

3 Anabolic steroids
Seeking super-fitness

Anabolic steroids are different from most other 'recreational' drugs in that they do not have an effect for several hours and do not make the user 'high'. After several weeks of use, some people feel energized and euphoric and, occasionally, more aggressive and competitive. Anabolic steroids were developed to treat men who had low testosterone levels and they are widely used therapeutically. When people use steroids recreationally it is usually in an attempt to improve their sporting performance or to change the way their body looks.

A medal lost
German wrestler Alexander Leipold (on top) won the gold medal at the Sydney 2000 Olympics, but afterwards had to return it because a drug test revealed a high level of anabolic steroids in his blood.

Effects of anabolic steroids

SHORT-TERM	LONG-TERM	OVERDOSE
Increase in body size	Heart damage/attack, stroke	Increase in body temperature
Increase in strength	Liver damage	Increase in blood pressure
Increase in stamina	Young males: erratic spontaneous erections; height growth is stopped	Risk of heart failure and stroke
Euphoria	Adult males: development of breast tissue	Convulsions, collapse, coma
Increase in energy	Women: changes to body hair, voice deepens, male pattern baldness, menstrual problems, fetal abnormalities and miscarriage	

Six pack blues

We go to the gym, to get fit – get a six pack stomach, you know. Some of the guys there, enormous muscles! Well, a friend of mine got talking to them to find out their regime. They showed him this stuff they inject. They carbo-load, work out all day and inject this drug. Steve thought it was a great idea, but I'm not so sure. I mean it's a drug, it's got side effects and there's more to life than the gym. I hope he's OK. He's a good mate. (John, 16 years old)

Anabolic steroids are usually taken in the form of tablets or injections. They are not addictive, though some people do become psychologically reliant on them. Long-term use of anabolic steroids carries some hefty health risks, including sudden death from heart attack or

CHAPTER 3

Cancer concern
American footballer Lyle Alzado blamed overuse of anabolic steroids for his brain cancer (from which he died in 1991).

stroke. Steroids also stop your bones growing, which can be a problem if you take them before you reach your full height. Stopping use can result in tiredness, mood swings and depression.

Anabolic steroids started to be used by Eastern European sports men and women in the 1950s and their use soon spread to other athletes. In 1976, the drugs were banned from the majority of sporting arenas. Since then a cat and mouse game has developed with the sporting authorities developing new tests, including blood tests at the Sydney 2000 Olympic Games, and some athletes developing new methods of masking their use. The problem is that with modern training methods, athletes are all super-fit and the differences between them are down to hundredths of a second. Therefore, anything that would give an athlete a slight edge over their competitors can be very attractive.

Fighting the case
Not all athletes accused of taking anabolic steroids are guilty. British runner Diane Modahl successfully challenged a positive drugs test by showing that mistakes at the laboratory testing her urine sample made the results unreliable.

4 Tranquillizers and sedatives
Uses and abuses

Tranquillizers, sedatives and drugs like 'easy lay' tend to have similar effects. They make you feel 'mellow' and relaxed and they reduce anxiety. Their effect lasts from a few hours to a few days.

Tranquillizers and barbiturates sprang to fame in the 1950s and 1960s, when they were used to treat anxiety, stress and depression-related disorders often experienced by lonely mothers at home. The drugs were nicknamed 'mothers' little helpers'. Many people became addicted and, because barbiturates can be lethal when mixed with

A tragic waste
Jimi Hendrix, one of the most talented rock guitarists of the 1960s, died from inhaling his own vomit after taking barbiturates in 1970. He was 27 years old.

alcohol, cases of overdose and suicide rocketed. Since then, newer, safer drugs have been developed and doctors have changed the way they use tranquillizers and barbiturates to minimize the risk of people becoming addicted to them.

Tranquillizers and sedatives are very useful drugs when prescribed appropriately by a doctor and when their use is closely monitored. They provide relief for people in great distress. However, the drugs are physically and psychologically addictive. People who use them can also develop a tolerance to them, which means that they have to have a higher dose to achieve the same effect.

Occasionally, tranquillizers and sedatives have the opposite effect to the one expected. Sometimes users find that instead of becoming relaxed and calm they become over-stimulated and experience anxiety, anger, rage and nightmares.

The effect of all tranquillizers and sedatives is increased with alcohol and at high doses this can result in the suppression of the breathing reflex and death. People under the influence of these drugs are often uncoordinated and should not try to operate dangerous machinery or drive cars. Overdoses of tranquillizers and sedatives on their own are not usually fatal but they can be dangerous when combined with other drugs.

Sedatives, tranquillizers and GHB

COMMON NAMES	CHEMICAL NAMES
SEDATIVES	
Barbs	Barbiturates
Downers	Amobarbital
	Chloral hydrate
	Glutethimide
TRANQUILLIZERS	
Jellies, Green eggs	Temazepam
Roofies	Rohypnol
Valium	Diazepam
Librium	Chlordiazepoxide
GHB	
Liquid X, Easy Lay	Gamma-hydroxybutyrate

Effects of sedatives, tranquillizers and GHB

SHORT-TERM
Euphoria
Drowsiness
Slurred speech
Uncoordinated muscle movement
Loss or impairment of memory
Poor learning ability
Occasionally: anxiety, nightmares, anger, hostility

GHB: drowsiness, nausea, vomiting, headaches

LONG-TERM
Depression
Loss of strength
Tiredness

Large doses of barbiturates interfere
with breathing

Chloral hydrate: linked to sudden death
and liver damage

When used therapeutically, tranquillizers and sedatives are usually taken in the form of tablets. But people who abuse the drugs often crush and dissolve the tablets and inject them, because their effect is then more dramatic. Recreational drug users might take tranquillizers and sedatives in this way, as a cheaper alternative to heroin and alcohol.

Date rape

Loss of memory (amnesia) is a side effect of some tranquillizers and sedatives that has led to a worrying development in the use of such drugs. Over the last few years, there have been increasing reports of a new crime, which has become known as 'Date Rape'. Drugs such as 'Easy Lay' and Roofies are sometimes slipped into the drinks of unwary victims. Like most other tranquillizers, their effect is to make the taker weak, dizzy, light-headed and mentally confused. In addition, they have a marked impact on memory, stopping or restricting the formation of new memories. The person who has been given the drug therefore becomes unable to resist when she or he is robbed, abused or raped by the attacker; and afterwards cannot remember completely what happened.

Be wary

Some sedatives are easily dissolved into drinks. Be very wary of accepting drinks from other people and don't leave your glass unattended.

To prevent this happening to you while you are out on the town, you should always go out with a group of friends and then look out for each other. Never accept drinks from strangers or even friends you are not completely sure of. Anyone beginning to show signs of dizziness and mental confusion should be given medical attention. Overdose is very easy when an alcoholic drink is spiked with sedative drugs, as the action of the drug is increased by alcohol. Drowsiness can often lead quickly to loss of consciousness, loss of reflexes and death.

A friend in need

You never think it's going to happen to you, do you? Well, I didn't. We had had all those talks at school, and Dad was always telling me to take care. Anyway, we go out clubbing on a Saturday night, locally, and this night about six of us had gone out as usual and met some blokes at the club. We'd seen them a few times before. I didn't think they were dangerous, just friendly. One of them bought me a drink and we sat chatting while the others danced. I didn't realize anything was wrong but I felt a bit woozy and wanted to go outside. This guy helped me. I thought he was being kind. My friend Heather spotted him helping me out, got the others, and followed us. They caught us up just as he was helping me into his car. I was out of it by then. They stopped him and took me to hospital. He'd put something in my drink – a roofie or something, the hospital said. Who knows what would have happened if Heather hadn't spotted me? It shook us all. The police were very kind but there weren't any witnesses and it is very hard to prove. I don't accept drinks from anyone now.

5 Cannabis
Sedative weed

Forms of cannabis
In the foreground are three blocks of cannabis resin. Behind them are leaves and flowering tops of the plant Cannabis sativa.

Cannabis is a sedative drug with an ancient history. One of the first accounts of the use of the cannabis plant, written in China in 28 BC, described its cultivation for fibre and rope and also mentioned its intoxicating properties. The plant has many uses. Its seeds are used for animal feed and oil, and its stems produce hemp fibre, traditionally used to make rope, cloth and paper. However, it is the unfertilized buds of the plant that are most prized for their ability to make you 'high'.

The unfertilized buds of the plant *Cannabis indica* produce a sticky brown resin that is particularly rich in delta-9-tetrahydro-cannabinol (THC). There are over 400 chemicals in cannabis, but THC is the most psychoactive and is believed to be the main chemical that makes the user high. The buds, and sometimes the less potent leaves of the cannabis plant, are used to produce the dried herb, blocks of resin, or oil that are all sold as cannabis. The drug is then smoked (with tobacco in a joint or through water or alcohol in a hookah or bong) or eaten (in its raw state, or in food, especially cakes).

Common names for cannabis

Marijuana	Black
Hashish	Gold
Pot	Hash oil
Hash	Smoke
Grass	Spliff
Reefer	Herb
Ganja	Blow
Weed	Wacky baccy
Tar	

The green grass of home

I tried cannabis once at a party. There was a guy who had a joint and was passing it round, so I thought 'Why not!' I inhaled pretty deeply and spent the rest of the evening with my head down the toilet being sick! I don't know what effect it had. It was embarrassing. The others wet themselves laughing. They said it was the tobacco in the joint that made me sick. I don't smoke. One of them said he felt 'spaced out man', and everything was very funny. It certainly didn't work on me. I think they were having a laugh and had put in grass from the garden instead of cannabis. (Mark, aged 16)

People who enjoy taking cannabis say that it makes them feel relaxed and happy. They feel a mix of tranquillity, hilarity and drowsiness. It also impairs judgement in a similar way to taking alcohol, making it dangerous to drive or operate machinery. Some degree of tolerance does develop in people who regularly take cannabis, which means that they have to take larger doses to achieve the same effect. It is also possible to become psychologically dependent on the drug, though physical addiction does not seem to occur.

Overdosing on cannabis can cause panic, anxiety and a high heart rate. This is rarely life-threatening and can usually be treated by 'talking down' (reassuring) the person affected. However, extreme care needs to be taken, as there have been reports of children becoming comatose after eating hash cakes by mistake.

Effects of taking cannabis

SHORT-TERM
Relaxation
Sedation
Hilarity
Tranquillity
Lack of aggression
Impaired judgement
Increased heart rate
Flushing
Bloodshot eyes
Inhibition of memory
Inhibition of ability to learn
Hunger ('the munchies')

LONG-TERM
Impaired memory formation and learning for 48 hours or more
Functioning of immune system probably affected
Lung disease (similar to smoking)
High doses: decreased sperm count or irregular periods
Effects can last for up to 3 weeks

Amsterdam
In many countries, cannabis is an illegal drug. But in the Netherlands it has been decriminalized. Coffee shops and bars (like this one) are allowed to sell small amounts (5g per person) of cannabis under tightly regulated conditions.

When a person smokes cannabis, the 400 or more chemicals in the smoke are quickly absorbed by their lungs and within minutes directly affect their bloodstream, heart, brain and other organs. This process takes a little longer when cannabis is eaten, though larger amounts tend to be taken in this way and so the effect lasts for longer.

'The only people who would really benefit from legalizing cannabis are those who profit from growing it or selling it.'
(Raol, policeman, 35 years)

THC receptors

A fascinating thing about cannabis is that there appear to be specific receptors for THC in our brains. Cannabis is not the only plant to have specific brain receptors. We also have opiate receptors that regulate pain. Our opiate receptors exist because we naturally produce a chemical called an endorphin to regulate pain and stress within our bodies. So it would be logical to think that our cannabinoid receptors are a sign that we naturally produce a chemical similar to THC. Two main chemicals in the brain stimulate the cannabinoid receptors; they are anandamide and 2-AG. What they do and how they work is not completely understood yet, but it would seem that anandamide has something to do with feelings of tranquillity and 2-AG decreases the ability of the brain to use memories efficiently. Why we would produce a chemical that decreases our ability to form memories is unclear. One idea is that it may help us to block traumatic memories such as childbirth or a car crash, so that we get over them more quickly. Both these effects can be observed when people use cannabis. In fact, the negative effects of cannabis on memory and the ability to create new memories mean that taking it can result in poor academic or technical performance.

Most of the 'high' from taking cannabis tends to wear off within a few hours but THC stays in the body much longer. It has been estimated that as much as 50 per cent of the THC remains in the bloodstream for 20 hours. THC is converted by the liver into other compounds that also have psychoactive effects. THC is also stored in body fat, where it is released when the fat is used. Therefore, its effects can last several days and traces from a large dose of cannabis can be detected up to three weeks after use.

Cannabis Club
Some people, including the members of this 'Cannabis Club' in San Francisco, say that smoking cannabis relieves the symptoms of illnesses such as cancer, arthritis and glaucoma. But a judge issued a court order to close the club since the drug is illegal.

Should cannabis be legalized?

At present in the UK, cannabis is a Class B, schedule 1 controlled substance under the Misuse of Drugs Act 1971. Drugs in schedule 1 are deemed to be of no medicinal value. If you are convicted by a court of possessing cannabis for personal use, the maximum penalty is five years in prison plus an unlimited fine. If you are convicted of intending to supply the drug to someone else, of growing cannabis or of allowing cannabis to be smoked on your premises, then the maximum penalty is 14 years in prison, an unlimited fine and the confiscation of anything you are thought to have gained by selling or growing the drug.

Some people feel that it is absurd for cannabis to be a class B schedule 1 drug as it seems to be less harmful than many legal drugs such as tobacco or alcohol. Others feel that cannabis is harmful and therefore should remain illegal. The debate about whether cannabis should be legalized is long-running and complex. Here are a few of the arguments put forward by both sides of the debate.

Arguments for the legalization of cannabis:

- Cannabis is a naturally occurring herb with beneficial properties.
- Cannabis is not physically addictive.
- Cannabis can be effectively used to treat various medical conditions such as muscle spasm in multiple sclerosis, nausea connected with chemotherapy, the wasting associated with AIDS and the treatment of glaucoma (an eye condition).
- Cannabis has been used for thousands of years and has many other practical uses, including for making rope, cloth and paper.
- Cannabis is attractive to young users *because* it is illegal. Therefore regulating and legalizing it will have the effect of reducing the numbers of people who misuse it.
- In the Netherlands, where the use of cannabis is legal within well-regulated environments, only 0.2 – 0.5 per cent of those who try cannabis go on to become problem drug users.
- Cannabis is much less harmful than many legal drugs, including alcohol and tobacco.

Marching for legalization
People have many different reasons for wanting cannabis to be legalized.

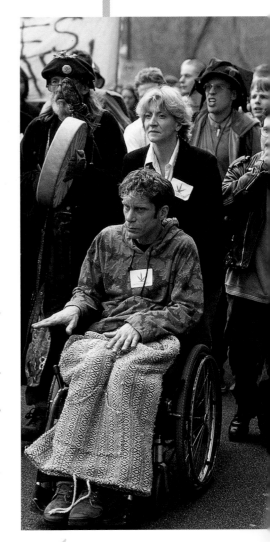

Arguments against the legalization of cannabis:

- Not all naturally occurring herbs are beneficial. Tobacco and deadly nightshade are both toxic herbs and whilst cannabis is not as toxic as these, it does have some negative effects on health.

- Cannabis users can become psychologically dependent on the drug.

- The medical uses of cannabis have not yet been fully researched, so officially the jury is still out on whether or not cannabis is a safe and reliable treatment.

'I don't know about legalizing cannabis. On the one hand it's not as bad as tobacco; on the other hand it still has its problems. It's tricky to know which side is right.' (Kirsten, student)

- Because a drug is a medicine does not mean that it is safe for everyone to use. For example, heroin is used medically to treat severe pain but it is highly addictive to people who use it recreationally.

- There are two main species of cannabis plant: *Cannabis sativa* and *Cannabis indica*. *Cannabis sativa* grows very tall, producing long fibres suitable for cloth- and paper-making. It is farmed in many parts of the world. *Cannabis indica* is grown mainly for its psychoactive properties. It is shorter, making it less suitable for commercial use in rope or paper. So in order to use hemp fibre there is no need to grow the variety of cannabis used to get high.

- If you legalize cannabis, the people who try it because it is risky and illegal will move on to drugs that are more dangerous, in order to be daring.

- Legalizing the drug would cause a big rise in its use and therefore a big increase in the amount spent on health care to deal with diseases associated with smoking it.

A useful plant

The cannabis plant has many practical uses – but people disagree about whether this is an argument for legalizing the drug.

6 Ecstasy
Happiness with a price

Ecstasy is a stimulant drug which was developed during research into the production of synthetic amphetamines (see page 45) in the 1930s. It was originally intended for use as an appetite suppressant. In the 1980s it was 'rediscovered' and used by some psychotherapists in couples' therapy sessions. The idea was that the sense of empathy and openness promoted by the drug would help couples to resolve problems. This hope was short-lived, however, as it proved very difficult to control the drug experience.

Common names for ecstasy
X
XTC
Adam
E

The chemical name is Methylenedioxymethamphetamine (MDMA).

Smuggled drugs
French customs officers foil an attempt to smuggle 358,000 ecstasy tablets into Britain. Ecstasy is often manufactured in makeshift laboratories and smuggled to its point of sale.

Now used as a recreational drug, ecstasy is usually sold in the form of tablets, which are swallowed or occasionally dissolved in water and injected. Ecstasy works by increasing the levels of neurotransmitters in your brain, so that your nervous system is stimulated and becomes very excited. The neurotransmitters affected include dopamine (which is one of the chemicals in your brain that regulate feelings of pleasure), noradrenalin (which heightens concentration on the here and now) and serotonin (which regulates sleep, mood and appetite).

Ecstasy acts differently from other stimulants, in that it seems to cause the release of lots of serotonin. The effects of this huge surge in serotonin production are not fully understood yet, but the result on the taker's mood is obvious. They feel happy, connected and full of empathy. However there are some major drawbacks to using ecstasy. One problem has only recently come to light. It seems that people who have taken high doses of ecstasy or taken it regularly for a number of years can develop panic attacks and depression problems. Animal studies have shown that high doses of ecstasy and prolonged exposure can result in permanent damage to the production of serotonin. This is very serious, as nerve damage cannot be repaired. So, people using ecstasy run the risk of irreversible changes to their brains. The research continues.

Ecstasy can be extremely dangerous in high doses. It can cause jitteriness, life-threateningly high temperature, muscle destruction, kidney failure, seizures and exhaustion. Long-term use of high doses of ecstasy can also result in the person experiencing hallucinations and paranoid psychotic symptoms.

Deadly variant of ecstasy arrives in Britain

15 men charged

Federal prosecutors charged 15 men yesterday, including a man they called the head bouncer at a Manhattan nightclub, for involvement in a scheme to sell thousands of dollars worth of Ecstasy and other drugs inside the club and at other locations ...

Ecstasy deaths

AN AVERAGE of 11 people die in Britain each year as a result of taking Ecstasy, according to figures published in February by the Office for National Statistics. The figure has been falling since 1994 when it reached a peak of 27. Ecstasy is also held responsible for many more deaths in which it was taken with other substances such as alcohol. (The Times, London, 20 November 2000)

Ecstasy affects serotonin

AN AUTOPSY of the brain of a chronic abuser of the drug ecstasy suggests that it may work by causing violent fluctuations in the brain chemical serotonin. (New York Times, 1 August 2000)

Effects of ecstasy

SHORT-TERM	LONG-TERM	OVERDOSE
Empathy	Depression	Jitteriness
Good feelings	Damage to the nerve	Teeth clenching
Feeling connectedness	endings using the	Kidney damage
Energy	serotonin	Death due to high body
Alertness	neurotransmitter	temperature, high blood
Increased body temperature	Anxiety	pressure or kidney failure
Increased heart rate	Suppression of libido (sex	Dehydration
Increased blood pressure	drive)	

Ecstasy became popular in the 1980s. One suggestion is that its rise in popularity may have been related to the new threat of an AIDS epidemic. The idea was that a generation of young people came into a world where sex carried with it the threat of contracting the HIV virus. For underage people going to clubs where they were too young to buy alcohol, one tablet of ecstasy gave them feelings of empathy, connectedness and love for all around them that lasted for 3 – 6 hours. It also suppresses sex drive.

Ecstasy became closely associated with the rave scene and all-night dancing. However, problems with the drug quickly became apparent. Several deaths occurred among young people who used ecstasy at clubs and raves. These deaths were attributed to very high body temperature and

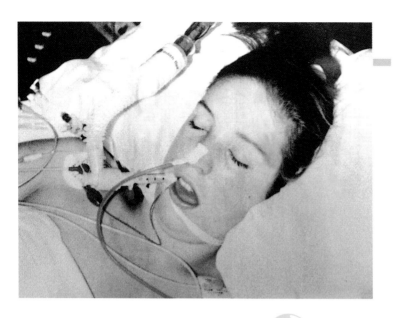

Leah Betts

The death of Leah Betts in 1995, from fluid overload after taking an ecstasy tablet at her 18th birthday party, made headline news in Britain. Her parents allowed pictures of her in a coma to be published, in order to warn other young people of the dangers associated with ecstasy.

dehydration. As we have seen, ecstasy is a stimulant and when you take it, you feel hyped up and ready to dance. However, the drug also raises your body temperature. The vigorous exercise of dancing can then push your temperature up to dangerous levels. These effects were being experienced in an environment that was hot and crowded and where adequate drinks were expensive or difficult to obtain. Some dance venues even charged very high prices for a drink of water.

These days most clubs provide 'chill out' rooms and free water. However there are still unscrupulous organizers of clubs who do not try to minimize the danger and there are even more unscrupulous drug dealers who supply tablets of dubious quality and strength or tablets mixed with other unknown substances.

Dealing with danger

I didn't think I'd ever do dealing. The penalties are so tough. I mean, it's not a caution or a ticking off – we're talking prison. I'd been doing Es (Ecstasy) at clubs for quite a while. Then I was out with my friends one night when one of them asked me if I had one spare. Well, I couldn't afford to start giving them away so I sold it. At cost price. I didn't make anything. But next time I scored (bought drugs) I got a few extra, just in case. I sold those easily so I got a few more and then more. I didn't push or anything – just got them for friends who were already using. Then one night one of my friends got busted (caught by the police) with gear (drugs) on him that he'd got from me. That gave me a bad few days. What if he told them who he'd got them from? I'd be looking at prison, goodbye college and good career. So no more dealing. It's not worth it.
(Kate, 19 years old)

7 Cocaine and amphetamines
Stimulant effects

Cocaine has a long history. It comes from the plant *Erythroxylon coca*, which grows in South America. Local people traditionally chewed its leaves to improve their endurance and experience pleasure. It was imported into Europe in the sixteenth century and then purified by German Albert Niemann. The pure substance is an extremely powerful stimulant and it was rapidly incorporated into a tonic wine and, eventually, into the original recipe of Coca-Cola. (Nowadays it has been replaced with caffeine.)

Coca pickers
Picking coca leaves in Bolivia. The leaves are then dried and processed into cocaine powder.

Psychologist Sigmund Freud helped to make cocaine fashionable among rich Europeans in the early twentieth century. In the tradition of the time, he experimented with the drug himself and enjoyed its effects. He mentioned the painkilling effects of cocaine to a friend, ophthalmologist Carl Koller, who went on to develop the use of cocaine as an anaesthetic for eye, nose and ear operations. However, the severe drawbacks of cocaine soon became apparent. It is extremely addictive. Because of the growing addiction problems, legal restrictions on the use of cocaine came into force around the world in the early twentieth century.

In the mid-1980s a new form of cocaine became available, called crack or freebase. It was created by purifying cocaine even further into a form that could easily be absorbed into the body by inhalation. Crack and freebase cocaine are very strong and extremely addictive. Even short periods of use can result in profound mental disorders such as paranoia, delusions and psychosis.

Amphetamines were developed as a result of work on a Chinese drug known as Mahuang, which was very good in helping breathing problems. Mahuang was found to contain a substance called ephedrine, and so the drug developers set out to produce a synthetic form of this. The first amphetamine to be synthesized was Benzedrine, which not only helped breathing, but also produced stimulation and euphoria. Abuse of and addiction to Benzedrine spread rapidly during the 1930s. More amphetamines were developed, appearing in pill form in time to be available to help soldiers stay awake during the Second World War. Since then, amphetamines have gone on to be used to treat conditions such as narcolepsy and attention deficit disorders.

Cocaine and amphetamines

COMMON NAMES	CHEMICAL NAMES
Coke, blow, candy, nose candy, rock	Cocaine hydrochloride
Crack, freebase, rocks, wash	Cocaine
Uppers, crank, bennies Ice, speed, meth	Amphetamine Methamphetamine
Crystalmeth Ritalin	Ephedrine Methylphenidate

Taking cocaine makes you feel euphoric and it is this feeling that makes the drug so addictive. Cocaine is usually snorted (breathed in through the nose), as it is absorbed directly into the bloodstream through mucous membranes. Amphetamines also give a sense of euphoria and are usually taken in the form of tablets (which are absorbed slowly) or inhaled as a vapour (which is faster). They make you feel confident, talkative

'People never learn. They go from one craze to the next;-speed, crack, the latest upper. It's always the same. They all screw you up.' (Abe, 30, drugs project worker)

and energetic. They depress appetite, eliminate fatigue and delay sleep. They literally stimulate the whole body, which can make them dangerous. They raise blood pressure, pulse rate and body temperature and if exercise pushes it higher still, this can prove fatal.

How the drugs work

All stimulant drugs, such as cocaine and amphetamines, work by acting on a related group of neurotransmitters – noradrenalin, adrenalin, dopamine and serotonin. The drugs increase the amount of all these neurotransmitters in the synapses. These neurotransmitters affect your experience of pleasure, stress, sleep, appetite and temperature. Your whole body goes into overdrive when you take stimulants.

Dopamine is involved in pleasure and reward. Firing lots of dopamine into your system will make you feel very good indeed. However, a substance that does this is therefore very addictive. Once you stop firing dopamine into your brain, the levels fall markedly as your body tries to restore balance. In the normal nerve synapse, a continuous recycling scheme goes on where the nerve saves its stores of neurotransmitters for using again. Stimulants actively stop this recycling action and lead to the loss of neurotransmitters. So, when you stop taking the drug, not only do the levels of neurotransmitters fall, but also there are fewer neurotransmitters available to replace them with. So you feel very low and miserable. Continued use of cocaine or amphetamines can drastically reduce the amount of neurotransmitters and result in the user feeling withdrawn and depressed.

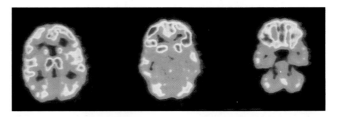
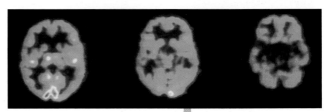

Brain scans
At the top are scans of cross-sections of a normal human brain. Below are scans of the brain of a person four months after heavy cocaine use. The yellow areas show brain activity.

Effects of cocaine and amphetamines

SHORT-TERM
Sense of alertness
Energy
Talkativeness
Sense of wellbeing
Increased heart rate
Increased blood pressure
Dilation of bronchioles in lungs
Euphoria
Profoundly addictive
Decreased appetite
Grandiose thoughts
Increased confidence
Increased activity
Violence (high dose)

OVERDOSE
Single dose can cause death.
Jitteriness
Headaches
Sudden cardiac death
Stroke
Breathing failure
High temperature

Cocaine: Seizures

LONG-TERM
Profoundly addictive
Exhaustion
Inability to experience
   pleasure except with drug
Ulcerated wounds – drug
   constricts the blood
   vessels around the
   delivery area
Repeated high dose over
   several days: psychotic
   state, hostility and
   paranoia
Repetitive ceaseless
   movement
Symptoms of paranoid
   schizophrenia
Violence
Atherosclerosis
Under-nourishment
Long-term nerve damage

Methamphetamine:
   mood and movement
   disorders

Born an addict

This baby was born prematurely and addicted to crack cocaine because its mother used the drug whilst she was pregnant.

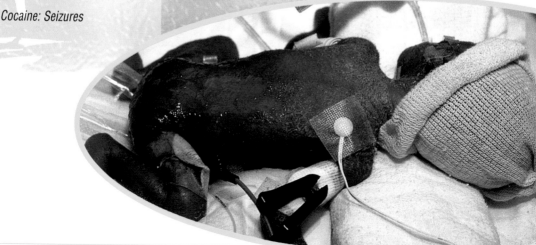

Obviously, the quickest way to stop feeling depressed after the effects of a stimulant have worn off is to take more of the drug. Addicts often report that the only thing that stops them taking cocaine when on a binge is physically running out of the drug. The good feelings they get when they take the drugs are reinforced by the lack of obvious immediate side effects. Unlike with nicotine or heroin, users don't feel sick or nauseous. In fact, cocaine is so addictive that animals that are given free access to unlimited cocaine will keep on self-dosing with the substance until they die.

Addiction to cocaine seems to be a result of refining the substance. It is not such a problem for native South Americans who simply chew the leaves. Tolerance to cocaine also develops quickly and rapidly reverses within a few days.

Withdrawal from cocaine and amphetamines, though an unpleasant experience, is not usually life-threatening. At the end of a run of amphetamine or cocaine abuse the person usually 'crashes'. They experience a period of extreme exhaustion, excessive sleep and depressive symptoms, a large appetite and hunger. They also experience craving for the drug. The most troublesome problem is that they have an inability to experience pleasure. This can last a few days, weeks or months and is a main reason for starting to take the drug again. The drug takes over your experience of pleasure to such an extent that nothing else can match it. Not a beautiful sunset, nor a delicious meal, nor love. Eventually this situation does improve, but getting through that patch can take an effort of great will. For long-term users the cravings can last for months.

No pleasure

The person in withdrawal from cocaine finds no pleasure even from the most spectacular natural scene.

Overdose is an ever-present threat for those who take stimulants and cocaine. There is a very fine line between a safe dose and an overdose and if cocaine is readily available users will keep on taking it and can rapidly push the levels of cocaine in their brain past the danger point. Both cocaine and amphetamines cause jitteriness, paranoia, hostility, violence, repetitive, aimless movement, palpitations, chest pains, high body temperature, flushed skin, headaches vomiting, stroke and heart attack. An overdose of cocaine also causes fits.

Speeding before a crash

My brother was fine before he went away to college. He never took drugs or anything. Then, during his finals, he just changed. I couldn't work out what was wrong with him. Nothing pleased him. He got thin and miserable and jumpy. Mum was so worried, but we couldn't do anything. It felt as though we were talking to him through a glass wall. He kept saying he was fine and working hard, but it was obviously rubbish. Then one night we got a call to say he was in a psychiatric hospital. Apparently he'd flipped out and started smashing some windows and acting weird. He had threatened someone. It turned out that he'd been using 'speed' (a stimulant) to study, to keep him going. His finals were coming up and he was desperate to do well. He'd had too much of the drug and it had done his head in. He's OK now. It's shaken mum up, though. She keeps saying it's her fault. It's hard to watch someone you love tear themselves apart.
(Oliver, aged 15)

Exam pressure
Like Oliver's brother, some people start to use amphetamines when they are studying for exams.

8 LSD and other hallucinogens
The 'mind expanders'

The most commonly available hallucinogens can be grouped into three main categories: LSD-type drugs, Belladonna alkaloids and Horse tranquillizers (PCP and Ketamine).

LSD-type drugs

LSD was first developed by a Swiss chemist called Albert Hoffman in 1938. He experimented with the drug on himself after accidentally eating a small quantity, and minutely recorded the first acid 'trip' (drug experience) in his scientific records. LSD was tested by everyone, including the American government. Psychology departments in universities around the world investigated the properties of the drug and it rapidly became popular with the students who tested it. LSD went on to become

'Acid tabs'
These pieces of paper are impregnated with LSD – 'the drug of the 1960s'.

The hallucinogens

COMMON NAMES	CHEMICAL NAMES
LSD, Acid, Blotter, Microdot	Lysergic acid diethylamide
Magic mushrooms, shrooms	Psilocybin mushrooms
Peyote, mescal, mesc	Mescalin
PCP, Angel dust	Phencyclidine
Special K, K	Ketamine
Jimsonweed, Deadly nightshade	Belladonna alkaloids

the drug of the psychedelic and Hippie eras (1950s and 60s). People took it for its mind-expanding properties and its ability to produce feelings of intense religious or artistic enlightenment. The drug was eventually made illegal in the mid-1960s and declared to be of no medicinal value.

LSD is usually sold on small pieces of blotting paper, sugar cubes, or microdots that are swallowed. It normally takes effect in 30-60 minutes and its influence can last for up to 12 hours. Once a trip is started, good or bad, it is almost impossible to stop.

The Merry Pranksters Bus

Ken Kesey and the Merry Pranksters took to the road in a psychedelic bus in 1964, taking LSD, playing music, performing street theatre and challenging the conventional. They are often credited with starting the Hippie movement.

People tend to notice few physical effects when they take LSD, but they experience profound psychological effects. The way they view the world around them is changed. Colours may seem more intense and sometimes people report mind-expanding or intense religious experiences. The experience is different for each individual and varies depending on time, place and company. Sometimes the distortions of time and space can be extremely frightening, often called a 'bad trip'. One to three per cent of people can experience extreme psychotic reactions to LSD, which result in them having to be admitted to hospital. Also, between 30 and 60 per cent of long-term users of LSD experience flashbacks (unexpectedly re-experiencing an LSD hallucination).

Staying in control

My mate offered me some LSD the other day. We were just hanging out and he said he'd got these tabs from his brother and did I want to share a trip with him. Well I didn't, really. There's enough mess going on in my head without releasing who knows what. I don't like the idea of a bad trip, or a good one. I want to stay in control. He said I was chicken, so I said he could take it if he liked and I'd make sure he didn't try to jump off any tall buildings, and take him to hospital when he got attacked by the spiders in his head. He didn't like the idea of that, said I ruined his 'karma'. He didn't take any either. (Jimmy, 17 years old)

Mescalin and psilocybin mushrooms are also included in the category of LSD-type drugs. Both have been used for thousands of years, usually in the belief that they will bring religious enlightenment.

Mescalin is still used during religious ceremonies by the North American Church and its use in this circumstance is protected by law. The drug's effects are similar to LSD's and can last as long. They are usually accompanied by severe nausea and vomiting.

Psilocybin mushrooms have a much less intense effect than LSD and their experience can last 2 to 3 hours. The main risks involve correct identification of the mushroom, as many poisonous varieties are very similar. These risks are higher when the mushrooms are dried, as it can be difficult even for experts to correctly identify a dried mushroom.

Belladonna alkaloids

These drugs have been used therapeutically for thousands of years, and doctors use them today to dilate the pupil during eye examinations and as muscle relaxants. However, used without medical supervision, they are very dangerous. The difference between the dosage needed to achieve hallucinations and an overdose is very small. An

Identification
Psilocybin mushrooms are not easy to tell apart from other, poisonous varieties.

Effects of hallucinogens

SHORT-TERM
Low dose:
  detachment from surroundings,
    emotional swings, altered
    sense of time and place
  increased heartbeat
  nausea, chills, numbness of face
    and lips, coordination problems

High dose:
  jitters, visual disturbances,
    hallucinations, illusions,
    possibility of a 'bad' trip

Phencyclidine and Ketamine:
  insensitivity to pain

LSD, mescalin, psilocybin mushrooms:
  separation from one's body, mystical
    and religious insights

LONG-TERM
General:
  acute anxiety, injury due to
    hallucinations
  dangerous when mixed with
    other drugs

LSD:
  flashbacks, psychotic reaction

Belladonna alkaloids and
Phencyclidine:
  can be lethal at normal dosage
  increased body temperature
  increased heart rate

Phencylidine:
  prolonged episodes of
    paranoid schizophrenia

overdose of these drugs will cause your body temperature to get dangerously high and can kill you.

Horse tranquillizers

Drugs in this category include PCP (Phencyclidine) and Special K (Ketamine). They were developed initially as general anaesthetics for use by vets. When smoked or eaten they produce a bizarre, drug-crazed state. They cause delusions, hallucinations and psychosis and insensitivity to pain, a very dangerous combination. They make you feel as if you are drunk and high on amphetamines and hallucinogens, all at the same time. They usually take 15–30 minutes to work and the effect can last for 4–6 hours and sometimes up to 48 hours. Using these drugs can result in prolonged episodes of paranoid schizophrenic-type symptoms.

9 Heroin and morphine
Drugs from the opium poppy

Harvesting opium
A worker in the Burma poppy fields scrapes raw opium from each poppy head.

Opium den
An opium den in New York, 1874.

Opiate drugs come from the sap of the seed head of the opium poppy (*papaver somniferum*). Nowadays it is possible to make synthetic opium products in a laboratory, but the vast majority of opium is still harvested from poppy fields around the world. When the flowers have finished and the seed heads are formed, small cuts are made on the side of the head and a brownish fluid gradually seeps out. This is collected, dried and formed into a ball known as gum opium. It can then be pounded into a powder and used directly or processed. The main active constituents of opium are morphine (very potent) and codeine (less potent). These can be processed into drugs like diamorphine (heroin), hydromorphone, oxycodone and hydrocodone, which are used therapeutically as painkillers and muscle relaxants.

The use of opiates was recorded in ancient Babylon around 4,000 years ago. They are traditionally connected with dreaming and the

The opiates

COMMON NAMES	CHEMICAL NAME	FORMS
Chinese molasses	Opium	Liquid (laudanum), powder – injected, smoked, swallowed
Heroin, smack, mojo, brown, skag, 'H'	Diamorphine	Powder – injected, smoked, swallowed
Morf, MS	Morphine, codeine, diphenoxylate	Tablets – swallowed or dissolved and injected

name morphine is taken from Morpheus, the Ancient Greek god of dreams. The Ancient Romans greatly valued the painkilling effects of opium and its use spread across the Roman Empire.

In the eighteenth and nineteenth centuries, China became famous for its opium dens, the opium equivalent of a bar or pub, where people sat or lay on couches smoking opium in clay pipes.

Laudanum (a mixture of alcohol and opium) was commonly available in the nineteenth century for use as a painkiller and cure-all and it was widely abused. Many famous people used laudanum, including Elizabeth Barrett Browning and Florence Nightingale. The poet Samuel Taylor Coleridge is famous for having created his masterpiece *Kubla Kahn* whilst under the influence of opium.

In 1898 the Bayer Company modified morphine to create diamorphine (heroin). This drug is absorbed into the brain much faster than morphine and is therefore very useful for emergency pain relief. However, the invention of the hypodermic syringe

Treatment
At the end of the twentieth century a pioneerng 2,000-bed detoxification centre was opened in the opium-producing region of China.

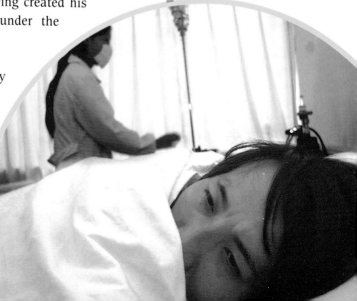

meant that heroin could be injected straight into the blood system. Today, although morphine and codeine are both abused, heroin is overwhelmingly the most popular street opiate.

Street heroin is a brown or white powder that is snorted, smoked or dissolved in saline solution and injected. It can vary from 10 to 60 per cent purity. It is usually 'cut' (mixed) with other less expensive substances like talc or even strychnine to increase the dealer's profits. The degree of dilution is one of the main risks of using heroin, as you can never be sure what dosage you are receiving. When injected, heroin takes a few minutes to take effect and the experience can last for 4-6 hours. Morphine takes about 5 minutes to take effect and lasts a similar length of time.

The American writer William Burroughs recorded his experiences with heroin and other drugs in the book *Junkie*, written in the 1950s. He said that heroin and morphine hit you in the back of the knees first, making you feel weak, warm, happy and deeply peaceful. This feeling spreads over your body and is often accompanied by nausea and vomiting. There follows a trance-like state

Damaged veins
People who inject heroin get badly scarred and damaged veins. This can result in serious health problems.

Effects of heroin

SHORT-TERM	LONG-TERM
Rush of pleasure	Constipation
Pinpoint pupils	Addiction
Insensitivity to pain	General poor health due to lack of
Flushed skin	personal care and poor diet
Nausea	Abscesses at injection site
Vomiting	Reduced immune function
Constipation	Cold and flu symptoms
Slow breathing	Injecting carries risk of HIV and
Trance-like state	hepatitis infection
Reduced awareness of the world	

OVERDOSE
Breathing slows then stops.
Can be treated at hospital (antidote Naxalone)

lasting from 2-6 hours, during which you feel no pain, cold, hunger, stress, anxiety or fear. All opiates affect your breathing reflex and slow it down. This can be fatal. If the emergency is discovered quickly enough, an antidote called naloxone can be administered at accident and emergency centres.

Heroin addiction

Opiates work by mimicking the natural neurotransmitters endorphin and encephalin in the brain. These neurotransmitters are involved in controlling movement, mood, body temperature, breathing, pain and stress. They also play a part in our experience of pleasure, which is why the opiates that mimic them are so addictive. In fact, the effects of endorphin and encephalin are so similar to the effects of opiates that they are often called natural opiates. It is these neurotransmitters that are largely responsible for

'If only people knew there is an antidote to heroin. They just need to get to hospital in time. It makes me so sad when young people die from heroin overdoses. Such a waste of a precious life.' (Jane, casualty nurse)

the 'rush' of pleasure that we experience after vigorous exercise or after sexual intercourse.

Opium drugs are addictive for two main reasons. They produce feelings of pleasure in a similar way to food and sex, but even more so. And they come with some nasty withdrawal symptoms, so that, faced with the choice between another fix (dose of the drug) and withdrawal, the person naturally chooses the former.

It is also easy to build up tolerance to opiates, which means that you need higher and higher doses to achieve the same effect. This can result in a rapid escalation of heroin use and addiction. In 1996, the average heroin habit was estimated to cost the user about £45 per day or £16,380 per year. It is practically impossible to hold down a job whilst you have this sort of heroin habit. For many addicts, the alternative is crime.

Addicts spend so much time trying to get the money to buy drugs, then trying to find someone to sell them, then taking and experiencing it, that there is no time left. Heroin addicts tend not to eat or care for themselves properly. Everything is centred on getting the next fix (dose). This, together with the depressing effect heroin has on the immune system, means that addicts get lots of infections and viruses. They have frequent colds and infections and find it difficult to fight them off.

Another health risk associated with injecting heroin is that of contracting HIV or hepatitis. One of the main methods of spread for these diseases is through sharing injecting equipment, including spoons or tools used to mix the drug. HIV and hepatitis are both killers, and in an

Needle exchange
Needle exchange programmes were started in the late 1980s, to try to prevent the spread of HIV and hepatitis among addicts sharing needles. Used needles are collected and replaced with sterile new ones.

effort to prevent their spread many countries have set up needle exchange systems where addicts can get clean needles. The only way to avoid contracting these diseases whilst using intravenous drugs is never to share any injecting equipment with anyone else.

The effects of withdrawing from heroin are legendary. Most have been exaggerated. Withdrawal without medical help can involve flu-like symptoms, aching muscles, severe cramps, stiff joints, sleep problems, feeling lousy, sweating, fluctuating temperature, runny nose, sore eyes, diarrhoea, headaches and craving. This is often called 'going cold turkey'. Well-managed withdrawal from heroin is not dangerous. Many addicts, if they survive that long, tend to stop on their own after 10 or 15 years of use.

Doing something right

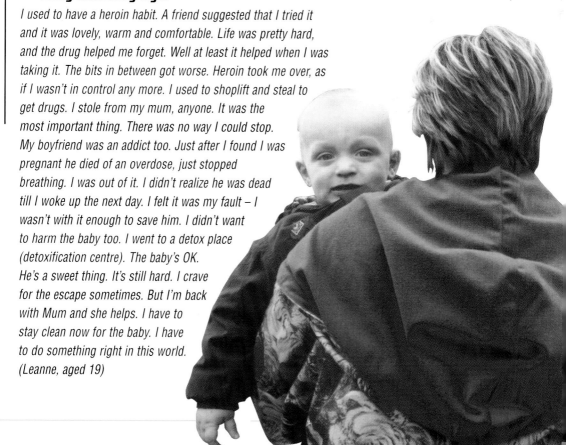

I used to have a heroin habit. A friend suggested that I tried it and it was lovely, warm and comfortable. Life was pretty hard, and the drug helped me forget. Well at least it helped when I was taking it. The bits in between got worse. Heroin took me over, as if I wasn't in control any more. I used to shoplift and steal to get drugs. I stole from my mum, anyone. It was the most important thing. There was no way I could stop. My boyfriend was an addict too. Just after I found I was pregnant he died of an overdose, just stopped breathing. I was out of it. I didn't realize he was dead till I woke up the next day. I felt it was my fault – I wasn't with it enough to save him. I didn't want to harm the baby too. I went to a detox place (detoxification centre). The baby's OK. He's a sweet thing. It's still hard. I crave for the escape sometimes. But I'm back with Mum and she helps. I have to stay clean now for the baby. I have to do something right in this world. (Leanne, aged 19)

Glossary

abscess   an infected cavity that forms in the body, filled with pus.

addiction   the repetitive and compulsive use of a drug despite its negative consequences.

addictive   causing addiction.

adrenalin   a neurotransmitter that regulates the body's physical response to stress.

angina   spasms in the blood vessels of the heart, which cause intense 'suffocating' pain.

atherosclerosis   porridge-like fat that coats the inside of blood vessels and makes them narrower.

bronchioles   tubes in the lungs through which air passes when you breathe in and out.

cholesterol   a chemical found in the bloodstream. Too much is thought to make you more likely to get heart disease.

cirrhosis   a serious form of liver damage where the normal liver wastes away and is replaced by connective tissue.

craving   longing desperately and urgently for something.

delusion   belief that a hallucination or illusion is real.

dementia   a form of mental illness where you gradually lose your mental abilities and memory. It is usually irreversible and accompanied by disintegration or death of brain tissue.

dopamine   a neurotransmitter involved in purposeful movement, hormone release, euphoria and the way we experience pleasure.

entactogen   MDMA and ecstasy are forms of amphetamine that produce behaviour so unlike usual amphetamines that they have been given their own classification called entactogen.

euphoria   an extreme feeling of wellbeing and elation.

fetal alcohol effects/ syndrome   a series of symptoms, including small size and impaired mental functioning and behaviour problems, that can affect babies born to mothers who abuse alcohol. When the baby is severely affected, it is said to have fetal alcohol syndrome.

hallucinate   to perceive something that is not really there. This can involve seeing, hearing, smelling, tasting or feeling.

hepatitis   a highly infectious virus transmitted by contact with body fluids such as blood or sperm. It causes serious inflammation of the liver and can be fatal.

high   slang for the experience of being under the influence of a psychoactive drug.

HIV   Human Immunodeficiency Virus – a virus that attacks part of the body's immune system. It is transmitted by contact with infected blood, sexual fluids or saliva.

immune system	the system in the body that protects it from infection.
impotence	inability to sustain an erection or ejaculate sperm during sexual intercourse.
inhale	to breathe in.
jaundice	a condition characterized by a yellow tinge to the skin and eyes, which is caused by high levels of bile pigments (used by the body during digestion). These bile pigments are usually disposed of into the digestive system, but if this route out of the body is blocked by gallstones or liver disease then they are distributed around the body by the blood system and cause jaundice.
metabolize	to break down food or drugs into a form that can be used by the body or excreted.
multiple sclerosis	a disease where there is damage to the myelin sheath that covers nerves. The myelin sheath normally speeds up the transmission of messages along the nerves. Damage to it slows down the messages. Multiple sclerosis causes problems with mobility, blurred or double vision, numbness, tingling and difficulties with bladder and bowel control.
neurotransmitter	a chemical that transmits a message across a junction (synapse) between two nerves. Neurotransmitters are mainly found in the brain and spinal cord.
noradrenalin	a neurotransmitter that regulates the body's physical and mental reaction to stress.
pancreatitis	infection and inflammation of the pancreas.
paranoia	a mental condition where you think that everyone is out to get you. Intense irrational fear and suspicion.
paranoid schizophrenia	a type of schizophrenia where the individual is deluded and feels either that a bad force is out to get them or that they are very powerful. They often experience hallucinations connected with their delusions and can be very jealous, anxious, angry and argumentative.
psychoactive	affecting your brain and behaviour.
psychotic	having a serious mental condition which usually involves illusions, confusion, delusions and hallucinations, with the sufferer not realizing they are ill.
sedation	a condition of being very sleepy or asleep, hard to wake up.
serotonin	a neurotransmitter that regulates your body clock, appetite, sleep patterns and body temperature.
snorting	breathing in a substance through your nose.
sperm count	the number of sperm released during one male orgasm.
testosterone	a hormone responsible for growth and male sexual characteristics.
tolerance	the ability to endure something without showing serious effects.
withdrawal	the process your body goes through when you stop taking a drug.

Resources

Books

C. Kuhn, S. Swartzwelder and W. Wilson, *Buzzed, The straight facts about the most used and abused drugs from alcohol to ecstasy*, W. W. Norton and Company, New York, London, 2003

Aidan Macfarlane and Ann McPherson, John Alstrop, *The Diary of a Teenage Health Freak*, Oxford Paperbacks, 2002 Funny, easy-to-read introduction to all health education issues including drugs.

Films

Blue Juice, 1995, directed by Bruce Kirkland, is a British film which tells the story of a group of surfers in Cornwall. It includes a 'rave' scene involving ecstasy use. Glamorized but interesting.

Christiane F, 1981, directed by Ulrich Edel, is a West German film following the story of a teenage girl as she becomes addicted to heroin (before HIV hit the headlines). Much praised for its 'no holds barred' look at the hard realities of addiction.

Trainspotting, 1996, directed by Danny Boyle, is a British film about a group of Scottish young men who experiment with heroin. An uncompromising look at the effects of heroin on their lives.

Withnail and I, 1987, directed by Thom Eberhardt, is a British film set in the 1960s. Two out-of-work actors try to deal with life through a haze of drugs. Deals light-heartedly with the choice between real life and living in a drug-induced fog.

Websites

www.ash.org.uk
Help and advice on giving up smoking.

www.mindbodysoul.gov.uk
British government site giving information about drugs.

www.re-solv.org
The society for the prevention of solvent and volatile substance abuse. Lots of facts and information.

Sources

M. Bloor and F. Wood (editors), *Addictions and problem drug use*, Jessica Kingsley, London, 1998

D. Emmett and G. Nice, *Understanding Drugs*, Jessica Kingsley, London, 1998

S. G. Forman, *Coping skills and interventions for children and adolescents*, Jossey-Bass, San Francisco, 1993

C. Kuhn, S. Swartzwelder, and W. Wilson, *Buzzed, The straight facts about the most used and abused drugs from alcohol to ecstasy*, W. W. Norton and Company, 1998

A. Macfarlane, and A. McPherson, *Teenagers, The Agony, the Ecstasy, the Answers*, Little Brown and Company. London, 1999

www.ash.org.uk (Action on Smoking and Health)
www.who.int/whr/1999/en/pdf/chapter5.pdf (World Health Organization)
www.homeoffice.gov.uk (British Home Office)

Index

accidents 8, 21, 25

addiction 9, 10, 11, 12, 35,
48, 57, 58
treatment of 9

addictive personality 11

alcohol 5, 8, 11, 12, 13, 14,
20, 31, 32, 33, 38, 55
and violence 23
effects 20, 21, 22
history 20
withdrawal 22-23

alcoholics 11, 22

amphetamines 40, 44, 45, 46
effects 45, 46, 47, 48, 49
history 45
withdrawal 48

anabolic steroids
effects 27, 28, 29
history 27, 29

barbiturates 30, 31, 32

Belladonna alkaloids 50, 52-
53

brain 6, 9, 11, 15, 19, 22, 23,
36, 37, 41, 46, 55
opiate receptors 36
THC receptors 36, 37

caffeine 14, 18, 44
effects 18
withdrawal 19

cannabis 6, 9, 11, 13, 34, 35,
36, 37, 39
effects 35, 36, 37
history 34
legalization debate 36, 37,
38, 39

chocolate 18, 19

cigarettes 14
advertising 16
deaths and disease relating
to smoking 15-16
(*see also* tobacco)

coca plant 4, 44

cocaine 4, 5, 7, 9, 15, 44, 46,
48
crack, freebase 44, 45, 47
effects 45, 46, 47, 48, 49
history 44
withdrawal 48

codeine 54, 56

coffee 9, 14, 18, 19

cold remedies 8, 12, 18, 19

craving 9

crime, drug-related 12, 32, 58

date rape 32, 33

diamorphine (heroin) 54, 55

dopamine 9, 10, 15, 22, 46
(*see also* neurotransmitters)

drug
bosses 12
dealers 12, 43, 56
smuggling 12, 40

drugs
addictiveness 7, 9, 10, 12,
14, 15, 22, 31, 44, 45, 46,
57, 58
deaths related to 8
effects on body 7, 9
effects on brain 6, 9, 10
effects on health 8
hallucinogenic 5, 50-53
metabolization 6-7

mixing 8, 12

poisoning 8

psychoactive (mood-altering
effects) 5, 6

recreational use 5

sedatives 5, 30

stimulants 5, 7, 14, 40, 41,
46, 48, 49

therapeutic use 4

'easy lay' 30, 31, 32

ecstasy 5, 13, 40, 41
deaths 42
effects 41, 42, 43
history 40, 42

ethanol 20

GHB 31, 32

glue sniffing 24 (*see also*
solvents)

hepatitis 8, 12, 58

heroin 5, 15, 32, 54, 55, 56
addiction 57, 58
antidote 57
effects 56, 57
withdrawal 59

HIV 8, 12, 58

Horse tranquillizers 50, 53
effects 53

hypodermic syringe 55

laudanum 55

laws on drugs 12, 16, 37, 44

LSD 50
effects 51, 53
history 50, 51

media, coverage of drugs 13
mescalin 4, 50, 52
morphine 54, 55, 56
 effects 56
mushrooms, psilocybin 4, 50, 52

needle exchanges 58-59
nerves 6, 9, 10
neurotransmitters 6, 7, 9, 10, 41, 46, 57
 adenosine 19
 adrenalin 46
 dopamine 9, 10, 46
 encephalin 57
 endorphin 57
 noradrenalin 46
 serotonin 41, 46
nicotine 14, 15, 16
 patch 16
nitrites 26
 effects 26
 history 26
 withdrawal 26

opium, opiate drugs 4, 54, 55, 57, 58
 history 54
 withdrawal 58
opium den 54, 55
overdose 8, 12, 31, 33, 35, 49

pleasure 9, 10, 15, 22, 46, 48, 57
'poppers', *see* nitrites

religion 4, 52
reward circuits 10
role-play 13

sedatives 30, 31, 32, 33
 effects 31, 32
solvents 24, 25
 effects 25, 26
 'sudden sniffing death' 25
smoking, *see* cigarettes *and* tobacco
suicide 8, 23, 25, 31
synapses 6, 46

tea 18
tobacco 5, 11, 13, 38
 advertising 16
 and developing world 16
 chemicals in 14, 15
 companies 15, 16
 deaths and diseases 15, 16
 effects 15
 history 14
 passive smoking 17
 stopping smoking 16
 withdrawal 16
tolerance 7, 8, 19, 22, 31, 35, 48, 58
tranquillizers 30, 31, 32
 effects 31, 32
'trips' 5, 50, 51

withdrawal 7, 9, 12

Note

Photographs illustrating the case studies in this book were posed by models.